1. A Special Child

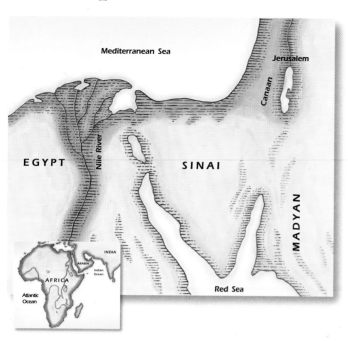

Yaqub ﷺ was the grandson of the great prophet Ibrahim ﷺ. He was himself a prophet, and also the leader of the whole tribe. He had twelve sons. Yusuf ﷺ was Yaqub's eleventh son and the first child of the Prophet Yaqub's wife, Rahil, who had been childless for many years. Rahil had one more son, Binyamin, Yusuf's little brother.

Long, long ago in a far-away place in Canaan, near Nablus, some thirty miles north of Jerusalem, lived a pious old man. His name was Yaqub ﷺ. He and his family and other relatives lived in tents woven from goat hair, and sent their animals to graze in the nearby hills and valleys. These were very fertile places, dotted here and there with little groves of trees. The pasture was so rich that they could stay for a long time in one place and did not have to move every week or so as some tribes did.

The Prophet Yaqub's family members usually spent their time looking after their herds of animals, milking their goats and sheep and making household things. Everything they did was to help and support their large family. Sometimes they would go out into the hills and hunt. Every so often they would load their pack animals with animal skins and meat and whatever cloth they had woven and take these goods to distant places to sell.

Tell Me About

THE PROPHET
YUSUF علیه السلام

S A N  Council   S

First published 2003
© Goodword Books 2003

Goodword Books Pvt. Ltd.
1, Nizamuddin West Market
New Delhi 110 013
Tel. +9111-2435 6666, 2435 5454, 2435 5729
Fax +9111-2435 7333, 2435 7980
e-mail: info@goodwordbooks.com
www.goodwordbooks.com

Illustrations: K.M. Ravindran

Printed and bound in India

بِسْمِ اللهِ الرَّحْمٰنِ الرَّحِيْمِ

CONTENTS

Yusuf's ten older half-brothers had another mother. As a child Yusuf ﷐ spent his time in and around the family, playing with his little brother Binyamin, running with the baby lambs and gazing out over the vast desert lands.

He had a keen intelligence and a kind nature. His father loved him dearly. He kept Yusuf ﷐ close to him, and had long talks with him even when Yusuf ﷐ was still quite young. From the very beginning Yaqub ﷐ was much impressed by this noble and gentle soul, for whom he saw a great and promising future.

'The Most Beautiful Story...'

The Qur'an devotes almost the entire twelfth *surah*, or chapter, to the story of the Prophet Yusuf ﷐. It is a story that shows us the power of love and compassion and the ability of man, with God's help, to find the right path in spite of all the difficulties and pain that may block the way.

Allah revealed this story to the Prophet Muhammad ﷺ at a time when his enemies, who wanted to stamp out God's message, had escalated their cruelty to the point of plotting his murder. It was during the last days of the Prophet Muhammad's stay in Makkah after the death of his wife Khadijah, a time in his life known as the Year of Sorrow. Muhammad was dispirited, and his companions and followers were in need of encouragement. At this difficult moment some of the Prophet Muhammad's opponents challenged him to prove that he was really a prophet by answering questions about one of the prophets of the Children of Israel whose story was not known among the Arabs—Yusuf ﷐. The Prophet Muhammad's enemies hoped to catch him making secret inquiries of the Jews about Yusuf ﷐, and then they would shout out loud that he was a fraud. As it turned out, they were disappointed.

The story of Yusuf ﷐ given to the Prophet Muhammad at this critical time was a lesson. and a source of inspiration for Muhammad and his followers. As the Qur'an says: "Surely in Yusuf ﷐ and his brothers there are signs for asking men." The story of Yusuf ﷐ and his brothers is very similar to the Prophet Muhammad's trials and ultimate triumph. The prophet's opponents in Makkah acted toward him just as Yusuf's brothers had toward Yusuf ﷐, and, like Yusuf ﷐, Muhammad ﷺ eventually attained a higher social stature than any of his opponents could imagine and succeeded in his God-given mission to establish the message of Islam.

2. The Sun, the Moon and Eleven Stars

One day Yusuf ﷺ had an unusual dream. In the dream eleven stars and the sun and the moon all bowed down to him. When he woke up, he hurried to tell his father about this strange dream. Yaqub ﷺ understood right away that great things lay in store for his young and best-loved son. This had been made plain in the dream. Sensing that his half brothers might become jealous of him and try to harm him, Yaqub ﷺ warned Yusuf ﷺ not to tell them about it: "My little son, do not tell your brothers about your dream lest they hatch a plot against you, for Satan is the open enemy of man."

Yaqub ﷺ cautioned his son, "The Lord has chosen you, Yusuf ﷺ, for a higher purpose. He will teach you to interpret dreams, and will perfect His blessings upon you." He told Yusuf ﷺ that Allah would bless him and their family in just the way He had blessed his grandfather Ishaq ﷺ and his great grandfather Ibrahim ﷺ.

The ten half-brothers were aware of their father's great love for Yusuf ﷺ. They would go off to look after the family's flocks, grumbling and muttering, and saying:

"Surely our father is clearly wrong." They were so jealous of Yusuf ﷺ that they would band together and fume and plot against him. But they did not dare tease him or hurt him openly, because their father was always nearby and would have been very angry. The young Yusuf ﷺ was innocent and did not even suspect his brothers' guile and hatred. The ten brothers not only hated their innocent younger half-brothers, Yusuf ﷺ and Binyamin, but they were disrespectful to their father, treating him as an ignorant old fool.

Yaqub ﷺ, of course, was nothing of the sort. Like his father Ishaq ﷺ and grandfather Ibrahim ﷺ, Yaqub ﷺ was a wise and noble man, a prophet who had been commanded by Allah to pass on the knowledge of the One God to the tribe and to the family. Some took heed of what they said and some did not; overall the family benefited from having such ancestors. But when Yaqub ﷺ tried to teach his own older sons anything, they would not listen to his words of wisdom.

The Meaning of Dreams

According to the Prophet Muhammad ﷺ you can have three kinds of dreams: you can dream about something from your heart, you can have a frightening dream from Satan, and you can have a dream that contains good news from Allah. The dream of a prophet is always a prophecy from Allah, which may be direct or symbolic.

The Prophet Yusuf's dream of eleven stars and the sun and the moon was a clear prophecy. One day he would be so much higher in rank that, when his brothers saw him, they would not even recognize him. And perhaps one day they would stand in need of him, and he would be in a position to help them, putting them to shame for their present plotting and betrayal.

But it is not always easy to interpret a dream, to tell what it means. The ordinary person could only guess, and as we shall see later in our story, even the wisest men of Egypt couldn't begin to fathom a strange dream the king had.

Only Yusuf ﷺ had that insight. He explained that his ability to interpret dreams was one of the gifts he was given by God.

3. A Plot Is Hatched

Finally the brothers' resentment reached the boiling point, and they went off to the hills where nobody could hear or see them. There they suggested something really outrageous. They said to each other: "Yusuf and his younger brother are dearer to our father than ourselves, though we are so many. Truly, our father is very much mistaken. Let us slay Yusuf, or cast him away in some far-off land, so that we may have no rivals for our father's love, and after that be honorable men."

As in their evil hearts they debated how to rid themselves of Yusuf ﷺ, one of the brothers who had a soft spot for Yusuf ﷺ

Jealousy: Satan's Weapon

The Prophet Yusuf's ten half-brothers were jealous of him, seeing his sublime personality and the attention and love that he received from their father. Jealousy is a base and poisonous emotion that cripples the heart. Only evil can come of jealousy, and that is why it is one of Satan's favorite weapons.

It is very dangerous to be jealous on seeing someone's superiority, or for any other reason. If allowed to grow, the seeds of envy can destroy even a believer's heart and soul. So, if you find yourself having feelings of jealousy, repent and pray to the Almighty to grant you refuge from the mischief of Satan. Jealousy is a proof that you are not content with God's decision and are ready to be guided by the Devil.

In that state of mind you are unable to tell right from wrong or good from bad. Therefore, the Qur'an reminds believers: "It may well be that you hate a thing while it is good for you, and it may well be that you love a thing while it is bad for you" (2:216).

spoke out against killing him. "Do not slay Yusuf, but, if you must, rather cast him into a dark well. Some caravan will take him up," he said. They all liked the idea and agreed upon it. And they knew where just such a well was to be found. It was deep and had completely dried up.

But now, for their plot to succeed, they had to deceive their father. So they made a plan to go on a false hunting trip outside the village, and all of them came to their father and pretended to be very sincere:

"Dear Father! Why don't you trust us with Yusuf? We certainly wish him well. Send him with us tomorrow, so that he can

play and enjoy himself." They assured their father that they would take good care of him. But Yaqub ﷺ sensed some mischief, and was unwilling to agree.

"I would feel very anxious if I let him go with you," said Yaqub ﷺ, "in case some wolf came along and ate him up while you were off your guard." But the brothers persisted: "It would be shameful if the wolf devoured him while there are so many of us." They convinced Yaqub ﷺ that ten strong, grown-up men would have to die before the wolf could touch young Yusuf!

Finally Yaqub ﷺ relented and put aside his fears, however reluctantly. What Yaqub ﷺ did not know was that the brothers did indeed have an evil intent, and that in saying he feared that the wolf might come and attack Yusuf ﷺ, he had unwittingly given an idea to the wicked ones that would help them carry out their terrible plan.

4. The Hunting Trip

The next morning, as Yaqub ﷺ saw his children off, he prayed for their safety and well-being, especially for his beloved son Yusuf ﷺ, who was about 16 years old at that time. Yaqub ﷺ was a prophet with incredible patience. He believed that Allah would be with his children all the time and would help them in need, although he did not know in what form Allah's help would come.

The brothers went deep into the countryside, taking their sheep and goats with them to graze on the hillsides. Yusuf ﷺ was cheerful, excited to be out on a trip with his older brothers. He ran happily here and there, and played among them contentedly.

Coming close to the well, they suddenly grabbed Yusuf ﷺ, seizing him from behind and grasping him by the arms and legs. He fought so hard to free himself

▲ **An old dried up well**
It was one such old well into which the Prophet Yusuf was thrown by his brothers.

that his shirt was pulled off his back. But no matter how he struggled, he was unable to escape their clutches: they were so much bigger than he was. They dragged him to the well and threw him down into it. He screamed as he fell, but they ignored him.

Although the well was quite deep, it had completely dried up. Yusuf ﷺ landed at the bottom of the well with a thud. He was dazed by the fall, but had no injuries except for some cuts made by the sharp edges of some stones on the inside wall of the well.

There would be no climbing those steep sides to escape. The brothers had run away, laughing and joking; they paid no attention to Yusuf's desperate cries for help. Without food or water, he lay there all alone for three days. He turned toward his Lord in the hope of receiving His help. Yusuf ﷺ may have been betrayed by his brothers, and left to die or to be sold into slavery, but he was undaunted. He put his trust in God, and his courage never failed him.

Allah revealed His will to Yusuf ﷺ, saying: "You shall tell them of all this when they will not know you."

5. "Sweet Patience!"

The evil brothers were busy now making another plan to fool their father. They killed a young goat and smeared Yusuf's shirt with its blood.

They waited until nightfall, before going back home to show that they had made an effort to search for their brother and save him. They pretended to be crying. "O father!" they wept, "What you feared has actually happened! We ran races and left Yusuf to look after our belongings. No sooner had we turned our backs than a wolf, seeing that Yusuf was alone, attacked him and ate him up." They produced his shirt soaked with the goat's blood as evidence. Yaqub's earlier fear about a wolf made them imagine that he would readily believe this story.

Yaqub ﷺ was utterly shocked and very distressed to hear this terrible news. He listened to the story about the wolf, but did not believe it. He was a wise man and could read their hearts. He sensed that there had been some foul play. When he examined the shirt, he saw that although it was bloodstained, it was not torn anywhere. In his heart he refused to accept the story: how

gentle the wolf must have been to devour Yusuf ﷺ but leave the shirt untouched!

"No!" he cried, "Your souls have tempted you to evil. Sweet patience! (*Sabr jamil!*) Allah alone can help me to bear the loss." Thus Yaqub ﷺ stilled his heart and begged Allah's assistance. For days he did not speak.

If the brothers expected to receive more love from him with Yusuf ﷺ gone, they were mistaken. Yaqub ﷺ spent more time in prayer and meditation. He asked Allah's protection for his little son. He consoled himself remembering Yusuf's dream of eleven stars and the sun and the moon. He was confident that Yusuf ﷺ must be alive somewhere and that Allah might have chosen him for some more noble cause.

Hardship and God's Plan

Besides demonstrating the unshakeable faith and highest degree of piety and righteousness of the Prophet Yusuf ﷺ, his "most beautiful story" offers several extraordinary lessons for the faithful.

One is that Allah always plans things that are for the betterment of the believer. Even if at face value something that happens looks like a hardship, it may eventually turn out to be a blessing. This is exactly what happened in the case of Yusuf ﷺ. He was thrown into a well, only to be taken to a better place. He was brought up in a noble family of very high rank in Egypt, and was given excellent training and education. He turned into a man of remarkable ability and wisdom.

But this can happen only if the person concerned endures with patience. The sweet patience—*sabr jamil*—shown by both Yaqub ﷺ and Yusuf ﷺ at the most difficult moments, sets a very fine example: the Prophet Yaqub ﷺ, having lost both of his beloved sons, merely turned to his Lord saying: "I complain to Allah of my sorrow and my sadness (*innama ashku baththi wa huzni ila'l Lah*)."

Despite being tricked and cast off by his brothers, being sold into slavery, and then falsely accused and imprisoned in Egypt, Yusuf ﷺ remained patient and truthful, and he kept his trust in the Lord. So Allah stayed with him. He did not forget him. He had a great plan for the Prophet Yusuf's future. But we are getting ahead of our story…

6. "O Good News!"

While his dear father sorrowed for him, Yusuf ﷺ lay at the bottom of the dark well, terrified because there was no way to get out. In the meantime, a caravan coming down from Syria and heading for Egypt was traveling through Palestine. In those days, people mostly bartered their goods, rather than use money. So they had to carry a lot of things, and these things had to be well guarded.

This caravan was carrying apricots, dried apples, figs, spices, balm and incense. It also carried woollen cloth, and some other goods. All of these things were packed in saddlebags carried by the camels, whose broad feet spread comfortably on the sand tracks.

Although the camels' movements were silent, there was a constant tinkling sound of their halter bells. There were also the long, low calls, made by the camel-drivers, one by one, as they moved at an even pace along the well-known track. They were expecting to reach the next well very soon, and when they did, the water carrier was sent off to draw some water for the animals and the travelers.

Suddenly, the water-carrier cried out: "Oh, good news! Here's a lucky find! A boy at the bottom at the well!"

Everyone ran across to see, and sure enough, there was Yusuf ﷺ, clamoring to get out of the well. They sent down a rope; he tied it around his waist, and they hauled him up. Imagine the travelers' surprise when they saw a good-looking boy with a face as bright as the sun! He looked as innocent as an angel, and had a very fine appearance.

Instead of returning the child to his family, they decided to take him with them to Egypt and sell him at the slave bazaar. They

reached the borders of Egypt and their journey was almost over.

Many, many years ago, long before there were cars or airplanes, when people had to go on long journeys across desert lands, they arranged to travel together in large groups. That way it was safer. Just to cross the Sinai Desert took almost two months, and there was always the risk of being attacked by bandits. They would walk, ride on camels or horses, or sit in wagons.

The whole group was called a *caravan*. To avoid the heat of the day in summer, the caravan would move at night. In winter it would travel around the clock.

The caravan, with hundreds of people, would move like a whole city under the leadership of the *amir*, who was like a ship's captain.

The caravan was usually accompanied by a troop of soldiers, with outriders and guides. To keep up their spirits, they sang as they traveled onward, and at night they stopped to build fires and bake their bread on hot stoves. Then they would sit around the fires, telling the old stories of their tribe.

In the morning they would set off again on the long slow trek.

Slaves in Egypt

In the days of Yusuf ﷺ, in Egypt and all over the world, rich people had slaves to serve them. People acquired slaves in different ways: they were either prisoners of war, or they were children who had been sold by poor parents, or they were people who, alone and unguarded, had been kidnapped.

Often slaves were able to earn their freedom, or their master freed them. Very often they became important people in society. Sometimes they became great scholars and leaders.

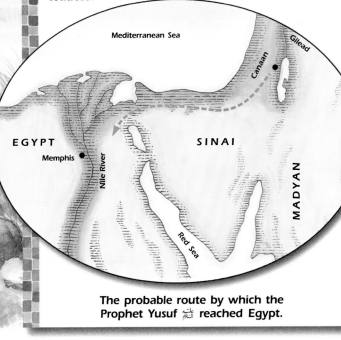

The probable route by which the Prophet Yusuf ﷺ reached Egypt.

7. Allah's Plan for Yusuf عليه السلام

When the caravan arrived, probably in the ancient city Memphis, Yusuf عليه السلام was sold for the paltry sum of 20 dirhams (small silver coins) to a nobleman, who took him into his service. The man who bought Yusuf عليه السلام was from the royal court and bore the title of Aziz (a title which was given to people of high rank such as governors). His name was Fitfir, or Potiphar.

The Aziz sensed immediately that there was something very special about this young man. Yusuf's handsome presence, his winning ways, his innocence, his intelligence and integrity, combined with his courtesy and noble manliness, greatly impressed the Aziz. A nobleman himself, the Aziz guessed that Yusuf عليه السلام must also be from a noble family. He, therefore, brought him home and instructed his wife to take good care of him, and asked her to treat him as an honored member of

▲ Ancient silver coins
The Qur'an tells us that the Prophet Yusuf was sold into slavery for just a few silver coins.

the household, adding that as they had no children, they might later on adopt him as a son.

Thus, according to Allah's plan, Yusuf ﷺ was brought from a small village to the most advanced city of the age to be trained and to carry out some purposeful task.

Memphis

At the time of our story the ancient city of Memphis was the largest city in Egypt. It was founded in 3000 B.C., when Upper Egypt and Lower Egypt were united. This was the beginning of Egypt's dynasties.

Ancient Egyptians described their country as being shaped like a lotus plant: the Nile River was like the stem, the Faiyum oasis was like the bud, and the delta was like the flower. Though Egypt's boundaries are much wider, that land is so dry and barren that very few people can live there. Egypt's population has always been clustered along the life-giving Nile, the world's longest river, which flows all the way from Ethiopia.

Once a year the river overflowed its banks. This was terrible for the people, because their houses and lands would often disappear beneath the waters. Even worse, the river changed its course every year when the waters were reaching their highest level. But the floodwaters also carried all sorts of earth and sand from further south, and deposited it on the land. This living matter, called silt, is a natural fertilizer that makes crops flourish. It was this, along with the water itself, which for thousands of years made Egypt one of the richest lands in the region. As a result, the Egyptians developed a mighty empire with powerful kings, who were later known as Pharaohs.

Memphis was located at the head of the Nile delta, where the delta joined the valley. It was an excellent position from which to govern both lands, and Memphis remained the capital throughout the Old Kingdom. By the time Yusuf ﷺ arrived in Memphis, some 1500 years later, the Old Kingdom had broken down, and there were a series of so-called intermediate dynasties, including several founded by invaders from the East, that ruled Egypt. In those days every king built himself a new palace and government buildings, so the size and shape of Memphis kept changing. But the major temples and the shipyards and harbor remained the same, and the city continued to flourish, and later had large foreign communities.

The city's name—in Egyptian, *Men-ofer*—means "established and beautiful." Indeed, it was. The city had grand buildings and temples dedicated to Egyptian gods. It had big markets and broad public squares. It was in one of these squares of this bustling city that Yusuf ﷺ was auctioned as a slave.

8. Yusuf ﷺ Faces Another Test

The years passed and Yusuf ﷺ grew into a handsome and charming young man. With his change of fortune in Egypt, Yusuf ﷺ grew in knowledge, judgment and power. The Aziz treated him with honor: Yusuf ﷺ was more his guest and son than his slave. He quickly learned the language and had become almost like an Egyptian. He was truthful and honest, so people asked his advice and respected his opinions.

This attractive young man fascinated the Aziz's beautiful and powerful wife, whose name was Zulaykha. Yusuf ﷺ kept his distance and never responded to her flirting, but Zulaykha would not take no for an answer. She followed Yusuf ﷺ around; but still he would not listen to her. Then one day when the Aziz was away, his wife found Yusuf ﷺ alone. She called him into her room and tried to seduce him. She bolted the doors and

The Gentle Voice of God

Yusuf ﷺ kept intact his divine nature, which saved him at this delicate moment. Allah has given every single human being this divine nature right from his or her birth; it is also called your conscience. It helps you to judge between right and wrong and to tell the difference between good and evil. Your conscience cautions you when you are in danger of going astray.

When you ignore your conscience, you are ignoring the gentle voice of God. You will not only be deprived of God's help, but will slowly weaken your God-given inherently divine nature. On the other hand, one who is obedient to his creator will bow the moment God's call is heard. God's help gives such a person the strength to stand up against any evil.

The righteous never attribute any good to themselves, but attribute all good to the great source of goodness—the Almighty Allah. For this reason man's self is called *ammarah*, meaning "the soul wont to command evil." At the slightest departure from the path of rectitude, *lawwamah*, meaning "self-accusing spirit," arouses pangs of conscience.

said: "Come!" The temptation was so strong that, if he had not been strengthened by his great faith in Allah, he would have fallen prey to mortal weakness.

Taken aback, Yusuf ﷺ said, "God forbid. My master has treated me with kindness. I cannot betray his trust." Yusuf ﷺ respected and loved the Aziz; he could not think of becoming involved with the Aziz's wife behind his back. Moreover, Yusuf ﷺ knew that it would be a sin against Allah. So, as Zulaykha fluttered her eyelashes, Yusuf ﷺ turned and ran toward the door. Zulaykha ran after him, caught hold of his shirt, and tore it. Yusuf ﷺ managed to open the door, only to find his master standing outside.

Zulaykha blurted out a wicked lie, in the way a guilty person often does, to explain herself to her husband and take revenge on the man who had spurned her. "What is the fitting punishment, my master, for one who has evil designs on your wife?" she cried. A moment before she had been showing her love for him, and now she began to accuse him falsely of misbehaving with her!

Yusuf ﷺ denied her charges, and explained that it was she who had tried to entice him. By this time a number of family members had gathered to find out what the commotion was about. One, who had probably seen everything, suggested: "If Yusuf's shirt is torn from the front, she is speaking the truth. If it is torn from behind, then it is he who is to be believed." The Aziz looked at Yusuf's shirt and saw that it was torn from behind. He realized that his wife was at fault. "Your cunning is great indeed!" he exclaimed, and cautioned her to ask Yusuf's pardon.

9. "Prison will be better…"

News of the incident spread throughout the town, and the womenfolk in particular began to gossip about it. They felt that Zulaykha was clearly in the wrong. The Aziz's wife invited the noble ladies of the town to a banquet, where she planned to prove to them that they would also have acted as she had. Giving each of them a knife, she told them to cut some fruit;

then she asked Yusuf ﷺ to pass through the dining room. When Yusuf ﷺ appeared, the ladies were so struck by his extraordinary good looks that they exclaimed: "God preserve us! This is no mortal, but a gracious angel!" And in great excitement they cut their fingers with the knives in their hands.

The women may have been distracted by the attractive personality of Yusuf ﷺ, but Yusuf ﷺ, by contrast, had his entire attention focused on Allah. He was so absorbed in the greatness and sublimity of Allah that no other thing was able to attract him.

▲ **Banquet by the Aziz's wife**
The Aziz's wife invited the noble ladies of the town to a banquet. Giving each of them a knife, she told them to cut some fruit; then she asked Yusuf ﷺ to pass through the hall. When the ladies saw him, they were wonderstruck and in great excitement cut their fingers with the knives.

The Aziz's wife did not change her attitude towards Yusuf ﷺ. She even threatened to send him to prison if he continued to reject her advances. Yusuf ﷺ prayed in great anguish: "Help me, O my Lord; prison will be better than what I am being asked to do. If you do not turn their plot away from me, I will incline towards them, and then I will be one of the ignorant people."

Even though the Aziz and the others knew that Yusuf ﷺ was innocent, they decided, probably to protect Zulaykha, to imprison him. That was unjust, but it was also Allah's answer to Yusuf's prayer. And, indeed, prison opened up another chapter in the life of the Prophet Yusuf ﷺ.

10. "O, My Fellow Prisoners"

The prison was dark. It was impossible to escape from it. There was no ray of sunlight. One could not tell whether it was day or night. But Yusuf ﷺ kept praying to his Lord. He remembered how Allah had rescued him from the dark well. He was sure that Allah would help him again.

Yusuf ﷺ had a clear conscience. He was innocent. And therefore, he was no ordinary prisoner. He waited patiently for Allah to reprieve him. He felt being locked up in prison was a good thing, for it prevented him from falling prey to the temptations of his master's home. But there was another and more important side to his being in prison. It was while he was there that Allah called upon him to become a prophet, following in the footsteps of his father Yaqub ﷺ, his grandfather Ishaq ﷺ and great grandfather Ibrahim ﷺ.

Yusuf ﷺ began his mission by bringing the word of Allah to the other inmates. He begged criminals to change their ways and sympathized with those who had been wrongly convicted. He advised them to put up with their suffering as patiently as they could.

> I have abandoned the ways of a people who do not believe in Allah and who even deny the hereafter. And I follow the ways of my fathers, Ibrahim ﷺ, Ishaq ﷺ and Yaqub ﷺ; and never could we attribute any partners whatever to Allah. That is a result of the grace of Allah to us and to all mankind; yet most men do not give thanks (12:37-38).

He felt that it was the right time to teach them the true faith. So he taught them to believe in the one true God and told them to give up their old, evil ways of idol worship:

"Fellow prisoners! Are diverse Lords better, or Allah the One, the Almighty? Those you worship besides Him are nothing but names that you and your fathers have devised and for which Allah has revealed no sanction. Judgment rests only with Allah. He has commanded you to worship none but Him. That is the true faith: yet most men do not know it"(12:39-40).

The Most Noble Prophet

Prophet Muhammad ﷺ met Yusuf عليه السلام on the occasion of the Miraculous Night Journey, or Isra, when the angel Jibril, sent by Allah, took the Prophet Muhammad ﷺ from Makkah to Jerusalem and from there through the heavens until he was in the presence of his Creator. On that incredible night the messenger of Allah met all of the prophets, including Yusuf عليه السلام, and led them in prayer. Muhammad ﷺ later said that the noblest of them all was Yusuf عليه السلام, because he was a prophet from a long line of prophets—Yaqub عليه السلام, Ishaq عليه السلام and Ibrahim عليه السلام.

11. Interpreting Dreams

There were two prisoners who entered the prison at the same time as Yusuf ﷺ. Both were servants in the royal court who had displeased the king. One of them was the king's cupbearer. His job was to serve wine to the king. The other was the king's baker. Both were charged with conspiring to poison the king. Both were impressed by the Prophet Yusuf's honesty and wisdom. They trusted him and began to consult him.

One night both of them had strange dreams. They came to Yusuf ﷺ and narrated the dreams. One told him that he saw himself pressing grapes to make wine. The other said that in his dream he saw himself carrying some bread on his head that was pecked at by birds. They requested Yusuf ﷺ, "to tell us their meaning, for we can see you are a man of virtue." Yusuf ﷺ replied that they would learn everything before their next meal. He added that his Lord had given this knowledge of interpreting dreams to him.

After teaching them the faith, Yusuf ﷺ interpreted the dreams. To the first, Yusuf ﷺ

▲ Pressing grapes
The cupbearer, one of the fellow prisoners of the Prophet Yusuf ﷺ saw in his dream that he was pressing grapes. The dream was successfully interpreted by the Prophet Yusuf ﷺ.

24

said that he would shortly be released from the prison and would again pour wine for his master. To the other he said that he would be sentenced to death and birds would peck at his head. Not long after, the Prophet Yusuf's predictions came true. At his trial, the baker was charged with conspiring to poison the king, found guilty, and condemned to death. The charges against the cupbearer were proved false; he was released and returned to the palace to his old job.

▲ **Birds pecking at their food.**
The other prisoner saw in his dream that he was carrying bread on his head and birds were pecking at it. This dream was also interpreted by the Prophet Yusuf ﷺ.

Yusuf ﷺ had asked the cup bearer, to relate to the king his own case of cruel and unjust imprisonment. But the cupbearer completely forgot the request, and Yusuf ﷺ languished in prison for some more years.

Ancient Egyptian Art

The ancient Egyptians, a highly cultured people who knew a great deal about life and death, were skilled in art and architecture. Ancient Egypt's pyramids are the oldest and largest stone structures in the world. The first pyramids were built about 4,500 years ago, and the largest, the Great Pyramid at Giza, which is one of the Seven Wonders of the Ancient World, was built with more than 2 million limestone blocks, each weighing an average of 2.3 metric tons! Temples were also built of limestone. Parts of the temples were designed to resemble plants: for example, columns carved to look like palm trees or papyrus reeds.

The finest paintings and other works of art were produced for tombs and temples. Artists covered the walls of tombs with bright, imaginative scenes of daily life and pictorial guides to the afterlife. These paintings were done very seriously and beautifully, for the Egyptians believed the scenes could come to life in the next world. Temples were decorated with carvings showing festivals, military victories and other important events. Sculptors also carved large stone sphinxes, the statues that were supposed to represent Egyptian kinds or gods and were used to guard temples and tombs.

Craftsmen employed by the royal families and by the temples could make almost anything: carved figures and personal ornaments from wood, ivory, alabaster, bronze, gold and turquoise, harnesses and every sort of implement. A favorite subject for small sculptures was the cat, which the Egyptians considered sacred and valued for protecting their grain supplies from mice.

12. Seven Fat Cows and Seven Weak Ones

In the meantime, one night the king of Egypt had a very strange dream that he failed to understand. He called his advisors, courtiers and priests to interpret the dream. All the learned men of the land came. The king, told them of how in his dream he had seen seven weak cows devouring seven fat ones, and seven green ears of corn being replaced by seven dry ones.

Everyone tried his best to explain the king's dream, but none of them gave an answer that satisfied the king. Suddenly the cupbearer remembered Yusuf عليه السلام and his great ability to interpret dreams.

The king sent the cupbearer to the prison to meet Yusuf عليه السلام, and he Yusuf عليه السلام explained the dream thus: in the lands of Egypt there would be seven years of prosperity. The farmers would grow lots of grain and the cattle would multiply. But following these seven years of prosperity and abundance, there would come seven years of severe and dreadful famine, when crops would not grow, cattle would die and people would starve to death. These seven years would use up all the stores they had laid by in the good years.

"There is a solution to this problem," added Yusuf عليه السلام. In the first seven years whatever crops were grown should be mostly saved, he advised. In this way, during the years of famine they would be able to use the grain that had been stored.

Yusuf عليه السلام also foretold that after seven years of famine, there would come a year

26

when there would be abundant rain and they would be blessed with great prosperity. In that year the vines and the olive trees that had suffered in the drought, would be revived and would yield their juice and they would have the oil from the linseed, sesame and the caster oil plant.

The cupbearer took Yusuf's interpretation to the king. The king was very pleased, and ordered that Yusuf عليه السلام be brought to the palace.

Economic Life in Ancient Egypt

One of the world's earliest civilizations was born, about 5000 years ago, in ancient Egypt. Egyptian civilization owes its existence to the life-giving presence of a mighty river – the Nile.

The Nile's annual flooding deposited a wide layer of rich soil along both sides of the river that produced bountiful harvests. Year-round irrigation was possible. It was also the main "roadway" for transportation and communication.

Agriculture was the mainstay of Egypt's population of 1-4 million people. Farmers grew wheat and barley mainly, but also lettuce, beans, onion, figs, dates, grapes, melons and cucumbers. Many farmers grew flax, which was used to make linen cloth. They also raised livestock – dairy and beef cattle, goats, ducks, geese and donkeys. Beekeeping for honey was popular among some.

Manufacturing was done in small shops, with linen clothing and textiles the main industry. Small shops produced all the other goods Egyptians needed to live and work, such as pottery, bricks, tools, glass weapons, and furniture. Such things as rope, baskets, mats and sheets of writing material were made from plants. Egyptian women liked perfume and jewelry, and craftsmen were skilled at making these things.

The royal household and the temples employed architects and engineers and many skilled craftsmen.

Ancient Egypt was rich in minerals. Large deposits of limestone, sandstone and granite were mined to build the pyramids and other monuments. Tin and gold was also mined.

At the time of our story Egypt did not have a money economy. Goods and services were traded directly for other goods and services. This is called a *barter* system. Workers were paid in wheat and barley. They used a little bit of the wheat and barley to exchange for clothing, cooking utensils or whatever else they needed.

Egypt carried on a lively foreign trade with Syria, Lebanon and other parts of southwestern Asia to the northeast, and with Nubia to the south. Egypt traded gold, other minerals, wheat and barley, and also papyrus sheets for the wood, iron, horses, ivory, copper, cattle and spices that it needed but did not have. Caravans plied the land route to the northeast, and Egyptian ships sailed up the Mediterranean coast and up and down the Nile.

13. A Man Worthy of Trust

The king's messenger ran to the prison to fetch Yusuf ﷺ, expecting the prisoner to be overjoyed at the summons from the king. To his amazement, Yusuf ﷺ refused to leave the prison until his name had been cleared. After all, Yusuf ﷺ was to carry out the prophetic mission of Allah. For this important duty, it was necessary that any false charges should be cleared and he should emerge with a clean image.

The king ordered an enquiry into Yusuf's complaint and found that all the charges against him were false. The Aziz's wife and other women were called. "We know no evil of him," the Aziz's wife admitted. "Now the truth must come to light," she said, "it was I who attempted to seduce him. He has told the truth."

When Yusuf ﷺ learned about the confession of the Aziz's wife, he thanked

▲ The King of Egypt placed the Prophet Yusuf ﷺ in charge of the granaries.

Allah from the depth of his heart. "Now my former master (the Aziz) will know that I did not betray him behind his back, and that Allah does not guide those who betray their trust," he exclaimed. Yusuf عليه السلام was honorably released from the prison. But he did not claim this victory as his own. "I am not trying to absolve myself," he said, "for man's inner self does incite him to evil, and only those are saved upon whom my Lord bestows His mercy. My Lord is forgiving and merciful."

When Yusuf عليه السلام appeared before the king, the latter was very impressed by his extraordinary personality, especially his wisdom and truthfulness. "From now on you shall dwell with us, honored and trusted," said the King. "Give me charge of the granaries of the realm. I shall be a good and intelligent keeper," replied Yusuf عليه السلام. The king happily made him the minister of granaries and charged him with making sure that there would be enough grain to meet all requirements during the famine that was to come.

14. "Thus We Established Yusuf"

The Prophet Yusuf ﷺ was about 30 years old when he was appointed by the king of Egypt as his trusted minister to look after the granaries.

Allah had established Yusuf ﷺ securely in the land of Egypt. Sometimes it is the hardships in life that lead the way to goodness. In the case of the Prophet Yusuf ﷺ, when he was thrown into the dark well, it was apparently a great hardship for him. But the world is managed and governed by Allah alone, and He makes special plans for His servants. So the well became the first step for Yusuf ﷺ to reach great heights, taken as he was from a small village to the most modern city of that time in Egypt and ultimately finding an honorable position in the house of a noble prince there. Likewise the dark prison became a stepping-stone to the royal court and ultimately to the seat of power in the land of Egypt.

▲ **The Nile River**
One of the reasons for the prosperity in Egypt was the great river, the Nile.

Misfortune and failure in life are common occurrences, but coupled with a positive attitude, they can be turned into future success. By contrast, failure coupled with a negative attitude can only lead to more failure. There is no end to the possibilities for success in life for the individual who can take a lesson from failure. But life's trials must be faced with patience, perseverance and compassion.

The story of the Prophet Yusuf ﷺ is a great reminder to believers to put their entire trust in Allah and pray to Him in good times, as well as in adversity. As the Qur'an puts it: "With every hardship comes ease" (94:5-6).

The Hyksos Kings

The story of the Prophet Yusuf ﷺ most likely took place during the rule of one of the six Hyksos kings who ruled Egypt from about 1700 to 1580 B.C., after invading the country from the east across the Sinai Peninsula. The name of this dynasty, certainly foreign in origin, comes from the Egyptian *hiq shasu* or *heku shoswet*, meaning "rulers of nomad lands," or — according to the late Egyptian historian Manetho — "shepherd kings."

The native people of Egypt were Copts, by their own account the descendants of Ham, one of the Prophet Nuh's sons. It is believed that the Hyksos were Arabs who had largely kept to their Bedouin way of life, despite the fact that, before their invasion of Egypt, they were already well established in Syria. This would explain why the king in this story was later to place his trust in Yusuf ﷺ, and it would also explain the subsequent happy settlement in Egypt of Yaqub's family — the Children of Israel. The Hebrews, too, were descended from one of the many Bedouin tribes who some centuries earlier had left the Arabian Peninsula for Mesopotamia and later for Syria. The language of the Hyksos must have been very similar to Hebrew, which, after all, is an ancient Arabian dialect.

The Hyksos were as advanced as the Egyptians in many ways, and in military technology they were superior. They brought new and powerful weapons to Egypt. They made spear points, arrowheads and battle-axes from bronze, a copper and tin alloy that was much stronger and could be made sharper than plain copper. They made bows of composite materials: laminated wood, horn and sinew that were stronger and gave more thrust to the arrow. Finally, they had horse-drawn chariots from which to wage battle. These military advances contributed to Egypt's power later on. The Hyksos rulers established their capitol at Avaris in the delta. They exacted tribute from the nobility and landowners of Upper Egypt based at Thebes, but were careful not to disturb the culture of Egypt, and actually adopted many of the local ways. They learned and used hieroglyphic writing and used traditional Egyptian titles in their royal court. They were accepted as legitimate rulers by many Egyptians and ruled for about 100 years.

But in Upper Egypt resentment over "foreign" domination continued to boil, and finally in 1560 BC, Ahmose I of Thebes began the decisive campaign that would capture Memphis and ultimately take over the Hyksos capitol of Avaris, driving the Hyksos back across the Sinai to Palestine.

15. The Famine in Egypt

Yusuf ﷺ set about his important duties. As second in command to the king, and with the blessings of Almighty Allah, Yusuf ﷺ traveled the length and breadth of Egypt. In every city he gave orders for huge storage buildings to be put up, to hold grain.

Recognizing his power and his talent for organization, people in all of Egypt's cities were glad to do as he bade. For seven whole years, they amassed plentiful harvests. There was grain without measure, piling up until it was like the sands of the desert. It was loaded on to carts to be dispatched to places where it was most needed and also sent down the river by barge from the great Nile delta. The granaries were gradually filling up, for Yusuf ﷺ had managed everything with superior skill. When the seven years were almost over, he saw that there was enough grain to see them through the hard times that were coming. He had successfully completed his preparations. The seven good years passed and the times of prosperity went by. Then came the seven lean and hungry

years, when no crops would grow. Now, famine held the land in its grip. The whole of Egypt was hit by it. The skies became white and hot and stayed that way; never a drop of water did they let fall upon the land. The land cracked, and the dry wind whipped up storms of dust. The Nile shriveled, people began to starve and animals began dying. Famine was everywhere.

Now, Yusuf ﷺ was busier than ever, distributing and selling the grain that had been saved and seeing that it was fairly shared out. Soon people from nearby countries, who were also hit by famine, heard that there was grain in Egypt.

16. The Brothers Visit Egypt

Many countries on the shores of the Mediterranean looked to Egypt as a source of food. Caravans came from all directions—from Syria and Arabia and the coast of North Africa—all hoping to buy grain or barter for it. Yusuf ﷺ had foreseen these countries' needs and had set aside enough foodstuffs for the purpose. But he restricted each trader to just one camel-load. That was as much as could fairly be given.

Back in the land of Canaan, Yaqub ﷺ and his sons were hit by the famine too. Like everywhere else, food had become scarce in their land too. When he came to know that people were traveling to Egypt for grain, Yaqub ﷺ asked his sons to go there to fetch some grain for the family, as there was hardly anything to eat. Only Binyamin did not accompany them, for Yaqub ﷺ could not endure being separated from him. He was very anxious about him—the only real brother of Yusuf ﷺ.

The ten brothers loaded their camels and began the slow journey to Egypt. After the long tiring trek, they finally arrived. Reaching the royal storehouse to buy grain, they presented themselves to the chief of the storehouses, the king of Egypt's minister. Although it had been about 20 years since he had seen them, Yusuf ﷺ recognized his brothers immediately. They — not surprisingly — did not recognize him. How could they have ever imagined that the young boy they had thrown down a dry well could have survived, much less risen to such a high rank?

▲ Ancient Egyptian plates, on which scientific information have been written.

Science and Technology in Ancient Egypt

The Egyptians made scientific discoveries and technological inventions to develop their civilization. These discoveries and inventions ensured that thousands of years later we would be able to know many things about what life was like at that time.

Mathematics was developed in Egypt to help with the economy and engineering projects. Egyptians could measure area, volume, distance and weight, and used a system of counting by tens. Mathematics was used to solve problems such as how much grain was in a granary, or how many bricks would be necessary to build a ramp. The amazing pyramids are testimony to the accuracy of their methods!

Medicine was also highly developed in ancient Egypt. Egyptian doctors studied the human body scientifically and could set broken bones, care for wounds and treat many illnesses. Some specialized in particular fields: defects of the eye was one, and stomach problems was another popular specialization.

A 365-day calendar was also devised using astronomical observations, to date events and keep track of religious festivals.

Even more important than development of the system of writing called hieroglyphics, the Egyptians produced the first kind of writing paper the world had ever seen: *papyrus*. The papyrus was a 10-15-foot-tall reed that grew wild in the vast marshes of the Nile Delta.

The Egyptians harvested this plant and figured out a way to turn it into lightweight but strong sheets, which were joined with flour paste to make long strips for long manuscripts, and could be rolled up as scrolls for storage.

The Egyptians used papyrus for all their record-keeping, including history and instructions for the souls of the dead that were kept in the tombs. Papyrus was exported all over the Middle East, with the result that other kingdoms and cultures were also able to keep records of their history.

17. "What More Could We Ask For?"

Yusuf ﷺ received his brothers honorably but did not tell them who he really was. In the course of conversation he asked about their situation and about the number of people in their family. They told him that they had old parents and one younger brother.

Yusuf ﷺ gave them enough provisions and treated them liberally—one camel load for each. The brothers requested an extra camel load for the brother who had not come. Yusuf ﷺ saw the chance to meet his younger brother, Binyamin, whom he longed very much to see, and explained that only those who were present could be provided for: "Next time, come with your brother. You have seen my generosity." An argument

probably followed, and Yusuf ﷺ said forcefully that if they did not bring their brother, they could be considered to be lying. He threatened that no grain would be given

Barter—an ancient way of paying

In the old days not everyone had gold, silver and copper coins with which to buy what they needed. Instead, they exchanged their goods with one another, sometimes giving a cow for several sheep, or a sheep for a bag of grain. This was called *barter*.

to them in the future if they failed to bring the brother whom they had mentioned.

"We will do our very best to persuade our father to part with him," the brothers said.

When they were preparing to leave, Yusuf ﷺ had their money and

merchandise put back into their packs. The happy band left Egypt with enough provisions for the entire year.

When they got back home and opened up their packs and found that their money and merchandise had been returned to them, they were thrilled with the kindness and generosity the king's minister had shown them. Their opinion of the keeper of the storehouses soared, and they were emboldened to ask Yaqub ﷺ if they could take Binyamin with them the next time.

"Oh father! What more could we ask for? Here is all our stuff — it has been returned to us!" they exclaimed to Yaqub ﷺ. "If you will just send Binyamin with us, we shall again be able to bring food for our family. We promise to guard our brother well."

But Yaqub ﷺ was reluctant. Though many years had passed, the memory of Yusuf ﷺ was still fresh in his mind, and he could not bear the thought of losing another child.

18. Trust in Allah

A year later, when it was time to return to Egypt to obtain grain for the following year, Yaqub's sons came to their old father. "Oh father!" they pleaded. "Unless we take Binyamin with us, all the grain of Egypt is to be withheld from us." The father feared for his son, remembering what had happened to Yusuf ﷺ. He asked: "Shall I entrust him to you as I entrusted his brother?"

But they went on and on pleading with him. Their persistence and the urgent need for food finally made Yaqub ﷺ agree to send his youngest son with his ten half-brothers to Egypt. But before that, he took from every one of them a solemn promise before Allah, that they would indeed take good care of him and bring him back home safely, unless they themselves were ambushed. They all promised. It was a serious moment, and everyone pledged his life to protect Binyamin. Yaqub ﷺ said, "Allah is witness to all that we say."

Then the Prophet Yaqub ﷺ advised his

▲ **An old city gate**
The Prophet Yaqub ﷺ said to his sons, "My sons, do not all enter the city by one gate. Enter it by different gates." He told them this to ensure their safety.

sons: "My sons, do not all enter the city by one gate. Enter it by different gates." He probably gave this advice in case the local people, seeing so many outsiders entering the city, tried to stop them. He added, "In no way can I shield you from the might of Allah. Judgment is His alone."

Though Yaqub ﷺ gave worldly advice to his sons to enter the city in small groups, at the same time he showed the utmost trust in Allah, saying that whatever happened would only be by His will. Then he prayed: "In Him I have put my trust. In Him let the faithful put their trust"(12:67)

To the sound of harness bells tinkling and the grunting of animals, the brothers set out once again down the long dusty road to Egypt. This time they were eleven, as

Binyamin was with them. They were now confident that they would be well received in Egypt and would be given all that they wanted.

They reached Egypt and entered the city in the way their father had told them. They went straight to the royal storehouse. When Yusuf ﷺ saw his younger brother Binyamin, he could hardly hold back his tears of joy. It had been more than twenty years since he had seen his brother, who was now in his prime.

Yusuf ﷺ greeted all the brothers, and then took Binyamin aside and embraced him, and confided to him that he was his lost brother. He comforted Binyamin and said he should not grieve over the past doings of their half-brothers. He also told him not to let anyone know about this.

19. The King's Cup

While the grain for Binyamin was being weighed out, Yusuf ﷺ put his drinking cup in his younger brother's packs. It was a gesture of great affection for his younger brother. Previously Yusuf ﷺ had done something similar when he put back into his brothers' packs all the money they had brought to buy grain. The brothers only realized this when they opened their packs once they were back home. This time too, no one knew of Yusuf's gift.

In the meantime, a measuring cup belonging to the king had been misplaced, and the courtiers suspected the brothers of stealing it. As the brothers passed

through the streets of the city, a group of royal guards rushed up to them and shouted: "Oh you people of the caravan! Indeed you are thieves!"

They turned back, and asked: "What have you lost?"

"The king's measuring cup is missing," a guard replied. "Whoever brings it back shall have a camel-load of corn."

"In God's name," they cried, "you know we did not come to do evil in this land. We are no thieves."

▲ **A precious cup.**
It was one such cup that was misplaced in the palace and it was mistakenly thought that Binyamin had stolen it.

But the guards argued, "What punishment shall be his who stole it, if you prove to be lying?"

The brothers said that according to the Prophet Ibrahim's law, which they followed, the victim of the theft would be entitled to take the thief as a slave in compensation for the crime committed against him. The guards immediately agreed. When the packs were opened, there, glinting in the sun, nestled a precious cup — in Binyamin's bag! This was not the cup they were actually looking for, but it was a similar one, a very expensive cup.

The brothers were terrified when the cup was discovered, but they showed no surprise, saying that Binyamin's brother Yusuf علیه السلام had also been a thief. Little did they realize that the king's minister they were addressing was none other than Yusuf علیه السلام! Yusuf علیه السلام showed restraint, saying only, "Your deed was worse. Allah best knows the things you speak of."

In this way the brothers themselves decided the punishment for the guilty party, and Binyamin was kept back by Yusuf علیه السلام. Under the king's law such a punishment was not possible. But this was not a trick on the part of the Prophet Yusuf علیه السلام to prevent his brother from leaving. In the words of the Qur'an, it was an inspiration, a plan from Allah: "Thus we planned (kidna) for Yusuf." (12:76).

A Providential Event

There are many different versions and interpretations of this episode. In some versions of the story of Yusuf علیه السلام, which also appears in the Bible, it is stated that Yusuf علیه السلام deliberately put the cup into Binyamin's bag to keep his brother with him in Egypt. Other versions simply say that "someone" put the cup in the bag, not necessarily Yusuf علیه السلام. Some interpreters say that it was the brothers who planted the cup in Binyamin's bag, to be rid of him as they had rid themselves of Yusuf علیه السلام before.

But in the Qur'an, two distinctly different words are used for the cups – clearly implying that Yusuf's gift and what the king lost were two different things. The drinking cup belonging to Yusuf علیه السلام is called *siqaya* (12:70), while the king's measuring cup is called *suwa* (12:72). The cup that was recovered from Binyamin's bag was a *siqaya*, not a *suwa*.

But the confusion between the cups was enough, and the guards' need to apprehend someone was sufficiently urgent for Binyamin to be found guilty on the spot. Ironically, the brothers had set the punishment, as asked.

It was truly a series of providential acts for Yusuf علیه السلام.

20. "Never Give Up Hope!"

Now the brothers had a serious problem. How could they face their father, who had taken a solemn pledge from them to bring Binyamin back? They pleaded with Yusuf ﷺ to free Binyamin: "Noble prince, this boy has an aged father. Take one of us, instead of him. We can see you are a generous man." One of the brothers offered to remain there as a hostage in place of Binyamin. (According to a tradition, he was the same brother who had objected to killing Yusuf ﷺ, suggesting that they cast him into a well instead.) But Yusuf ﷺ turned down the request: "God forbid that we should take any but the man with whom our property was found: for then we should be unjust."

The brothers were so upset they did not know what to do. The eldest brother refused to leave Egypt; he didn't have the courage to show his face to his father. He accused his brothers: "Do you not know that your father took from you a pledge in Allah's name, and that long ago you did your worst with Yusuf ﷺ? I will not stir from this land until my father gives me leave or Allah makes known to me His judgment." He asked his brothers to return to their father and tell him: "Father, your son has committed a

theft. We testify only to what we know. How could we guard against the unforeseen? Inquire at the city where we lodged, and from the caravan with which we traveled. We speak the truth."

When they reached home without Binyamin, the brothers told their ailing father that his son had committed a theft and that the king's minister had

42

kept him as a punishment. The brothers swore to their father that this was the truth, and they even made the people of the caravan bear witness. Yaqub عليه السلام was absolutely stunned by the story. He knew his little Binyamin too well to believe that he had stolen anything. He flatly refused to believe them, thinking they had plotted to get rid of their youngest brother just as they had

plotted against Yusuf عليه السلام. So he cried out, "No! Your souls have tempted you to evil. But I will have sweet patience (*sabr jamil*). Allah may bring them all to me... He alone is All-Knowing and Wise."

The loss of Yusuf عليه السلام and now Binyamin was so hard for Yaqub عليه السلام to bear that he lost his eyesight weeping. Ruefully, he thought of

how Yusuf's boyhood dreams had augured his greatness. For himself, the whole world had been plunged into darkness. He poured out his distraction and grief only to Allah. His faith was still as strong as ever and he observed the discipline of patience—the greatest virtue of the faithful.

Turning away from his sons, Yaqub عليه السلام cried, "How great is my grief for Yusuf عليه السلام!" The sons retorted, "By God! You will never cease to remember Yusuf عليه السلام until you ruin your health or die." But Yaqub عليه السلام forgave the sting and malice in the words of his sons and, like a prophet of Allah, he still wished them well, gave sound advice, and did not lose hope.

"O my sons! Go and enquire about Yusuf عليه السلام and his brother, and never give up hope of Allah's soothing mercy," Yaqub عليه السلام said. "Truly, no one despairs of Allah's soothing mercy, except those who have no faith."

21. "None Shall Reproach You …"

So the sons of Yaqub ﷺ once again set out for Egypt in the hope that the king's minister would agree to their request to release Binyamin.

Finally they reached Egypt, met Yusuf ﷺ and pleaded with him to release Binyamin. They told him that their father was an old man who deeply grieved for his son. They also pleaded with Yusuf ﷺ for charity as they had not brought much money this time. They said, "Noble prince, we and our people are scourged with famine." They had spent a great part of their capital and stock-in-trade. "We have brought very little money. Give us some corn, and be charitable to us: Allah rewards the charitable."

To their pleadings, Yusuf ﷺ replied: "Do you know what you did to Yusuf and his brother?" At once the brothers realized that they were in the presence of Yusuf ﷺ!

"What!" the brothers exclaimed. "Can you indeed be Yusuf?" They could not believe their eyes. "I am Yusuf," he answered, "and this is my brother. Allah has been very generous to us. Those who keep from evil and endure with fortitude will not be denied their reward by Allah." They may suffer a great deal, but Allah at last rewards patience and right conduct.

At first, the brothers feared that Yusuf ﷺ might want to punish them, but he treated them kindly. "By the Lord," the brothers said, "Allah has exalted you above us all. We have indeed been guilty." They freely confessed their wrongdoing.

But Yusuf ﷺ was such a kind-hearted person that he did not rebuke them at all. "None shall reproach you this day. May Allah forgive you," he said. The brothers were full of amazement, deeply relieved and grateful.

Forgiveness is a great virtue

Yusuf ﷺ pardoned his brothers instantly for the harm they had done him. He also asked Allah's forgiveness for them. Yusuf ﷺ was not concerned for his own sake. He was concerned only for his mission as a prophet, to call people to Allah and to bring them to Him.

When the Prophet Muhammad ﷺ conquered Makkah, he behaved in exactly the same way as Yusuf ﷺ. He took hold of the two sides of the gate of the Kabah and said to the Quraysh, the people who for almost twenty years had persecuted him and his followers: "How do you think I should treat you?" They replied, "We hope for good, you are a noble brother and the son of a noble brother."

"I say as my brother Yusuf ﷺ said," the Prophet replied to them, "Let no one reproach you this day." The Prophet forgave all his opponents, and thus a new chapter was opened in the history of Islam. All those opponents, who in ordinary circumstances would have been beheaded for treachery, ultimately embraced Islam and served its cause. It was the kind of turning point that has not been seen since in the history of Islam.

22. The Breath of Yusuf عليه السلام

Before the brothers left for home, Yusuf عليه السلام gave his shirt to them and told them to touch his father's eyes with it to restore his sight, and to bring his parents to him. (Remember that the brothers had covered up their crime against Yusuf عليه السلام many years earlier by taking his shirt, putting false bloodstains on it, and pretending that he had been killed by a wolf.)

As they approached their land, Yaqub عليه السلام sensed that they were near, although they were still some distance from home, because he could smell the scent of Yusuf's shirt. No sooner had the caravan reached their town than the father said: "I feel the breath of Yusuf عليه السلام, though you will not believe me." It was as if he felt the presence of Yusuf عليه السلام in the air. When a long-lost friend is about to be rediscovered, many people have a sort of foretaste of it, which they call telepathy. In the case of Yaqub عليه السلام it was more definite. But the people around Yaqub عليه السلام thought he had lost his mind. "In God's name," said those who heard him, "it is only your old illusion."

As soon as the brothers arrived back home, they gave their father the good news that Yusuf عليه السلام was alive and patted his face with the shirt. Yaqub عليه السلام at once regained his sight. He was overjoyed and, thanking Allah, said, "Did I not tell you, Allah has made known to me what you do not know?"

His sons sank their heads in shame and asked for forgiveness: "Father, beg for forgiveness for our sins. We have indeed done wrong." He replied, "I shall beg my Lord to forgive you. He is forgiving and merciful"

(12:96-98). Yaqub ﷺ did not ask for forgiveness for them at that very moment. He knew that there is a special time to do that — just before the dawn. That is a special time for remembrance of Allah and asking forgiveness. That is a time when Allah answers prayers.

The brothers told their father about Yusuf ﷺ, who was now a powerful minister in the land of Egypt, next only to the king. They also told him about his invitation to them to bring their parents to settle in Egypt.

When all the household goods were packed, and other useful things like tools and weapons, rope and looms were added, they rolled up their tents and threw them over the

There is charity in forgiveness

Abu Abbas ibn Hibr relates that one day the Prophet exhorted people to donate something towards God's cause, and people gave according to their means. One of the Prophet's Companions, Ulbah ibn Zayd ibn Haritha, did not, however, have anything to give. He arose that night and, weeping before God, prayed to Him: "Lord I have nothing to give to charity. Instead Lord, I forgive whoever has brought me dishonour."

In the morning when the Companions had gathered, the Prophet asked them, "Where is the one who gave something to charity last night?" When no one arose, the Prophet repeated his question. Still no one answered. Then, when the Prophet had repeated his question for the third time, Ulbah ibn Zayd ibn Haritha arose. "Rejoice," said the Prophet, "for your gift to charity has been accepted." (Al-bidayah wa Al-Mhayah)

backs of their camels. They herded their flocks together. Yaqub's family bade farewell to the land of Canaan, little knowing that their people would not return for hundreds of years, and moved off toward Egypt.

As they crossed the western expanses of the desert and approached the fertile delta of the Nile, they noticed many changes in the landscape. Finally, one of the brothers who had gone on ahead shouted, "The city! The city of Yusuf ﷺ! Our journey is almost at an end!"

23. The Dream Comes True

They were immediately able to see the rank to which Yusuf ﷺ had risen. Yusuf ﷺ embraced his parents and held them in honor. He made them sit on the throne and said: "Welcome to Egypt, in safety, if Allah will!" According to an old Egyptian custom, the place of honor at a ceremonial reception is on a seat or a dais, with a special cushion of honor.

Seeing the splendor and high position of Yusuf ﷺ, they all fell prostrate, as a mark of thanksgiving and awe. "This," Yusuf ﷺ reminded his father, "is the meaning of my dream, which my Lord has fulfilled." He explained that his parents were the sun and the moon, and his brothers were the stars!

Overwhelmed with gratitude to Allah for delivering him from prison, for reuniting him with his parents and for guiding his brothers back to the right path, Yusuf ﷺ prostrated himself before

Allah saying: "O my Lord! You have indeed bestowed on me power, and taught me the interpretation of dreams. O You Creator of the heavens and the earth! You are my Protector in this world and in the Hereafter. Take my soul at death as one submitting to Your will, and unite me with the righteous" (12:101).

According to Ibn Athir and Tabari, Yusuf ﷺ died at the age of 110 years, 64 years before the birth of the Prophet Musa ﷺ.